Steffi Graf

PHOTO CREDITS
Allsport: cover, pg. 2, 18, 22, 26
Wide World: pg. 9, 13, 17, 25 and 30
Ron Koch: pg. 6, 10, 14, 21, 29

Distributed to Schools and Libraries
in the United States by
ENCYCLOPAEDIA BRITANNICA EDUCATIONAL CORP.
310 S. Michigan Avenue
Chicago, Illinois 60604

Library of Congress Cataloging-in-Publication Data
Rothaus, James.
Steffi Graf / Jim Rothaus.
p. cm.
Summary: A brief career biography of the young German
woman whose powerful forehand and amazing foot speed make her
one of the best women tennis players ever.
ISBN 0-89565-734-1
1. Graf, Stephanie, 1969-   —Juvenile literature.
2. Tennis players—Germany—Biography—Juvenile literature.
3. Women tennis players—Germany—Biography—Juvenile literature.
[1. Graf, Stephanie, 1969-   . 2. Tennis players.] I. Title.
GV994.G7R78 1991   91-16393
796.342'092–dc20   CIP
[B]   AC

Steffi Graf

by James R. Rothaus

The biggest surprise in the 1989 French Open wasn't that seventeen-year-old Arantxa Sanchez won the tournament. No, the biggest surprise was that Steffi Graf didn't. The nineteen-year-old Graf had won every major tennis tournament in the past year and a half. Graf claimed the Grand Slam of tennis in 1988. She did this by winning the Australian Open, the French Open, the All-England Championships at Wimbledon, and the U.S. Open. Then Graf won the gold medal at the 1988 Summer Olympics in Seoul, South Korea.

When Graf didn't win the 1989 French Open, some people wondered if she could bounce back to win Wimbledon several months later. Those people shouldn't have bothered worrying about Graf. She turned all her energy toward winning Wimbledon. "There were times last year [1988] I didn't know how much I was winning and how tough it was," Graf said. "When you lose a couple of times, it makes you realize how hard winning is." Graf, however, made it look easy at Wimbledon in 1989.

Graf is hard to beat.

After losing to Graf in the first round, Nathalie Herrman just shook her head. "Even when you play good, it's bad," Herrman said. In the second round, American Terry Phelps knew she had little chance of beating the German star. "Wow!" Phelps exclaimed after losing to Steffi. "I felt like I was playing a guy. Unbelievable. Oh yes, I had lots of advice before the match. If I had seen any of those people in the stands, I would have shouted, 'Nothing works.'"

It didn't get any easier
for Graf's opponents in the later
rounds of the tournament. Graf had
no trouble beating Ros Fairbanks in
the next match. "You get the feeling
she knows her opponents do not feel
they can beat her," Fairbanks said
after the match. Whether Graf's
opponents believed they could beat
her or not, it didn't matter. Graf
served her way to her second
straight Wimbledon title. Two
months later, Graf won her second
straight U.S. Open crown. The
German had captured seven of the
last eight Grand Slam events.

13

Some players on the women's professional tennis tour started to wonder if Graf could play any better. "I don't know how much more she can improve," said Martina Navratilova, the second-best player in the world. Chris Evert, who was once the top female player, didn't agree with Navratilova. "With Steffi," Evert said, "I think the best is yet to come." One thing was certain. Graf would never stop working to try to improve. Tennis has been most of her life.

Graf was born in 1969 in Bruhl, West Germany. It is a small city in the southwestern part of the country. She grew up only a short distance away from another future tennis star, Boris Becker. In fact, Graf and Becker got to know each other on the tennis court at a young age. Both of them played at the same tennis club as youngsters. "I used to be the worst in the boys, and she was best in the girls," Becker recalled. "So when I was maybe nine and she was seven, I had to play with her."

Becker was a big boy who was kind of clumsy on the tennis court. Graf, however, was quite small and very graceful. Despite her lack of size, Graf had developed a powerful forehand. Opponents were shocked to see a little girl hit the ball so hard. "I played Steffi when she was twelve. She was so tiny I could hardly see her over the net," remembered Eva Pfaff, who later became a pro. "I couldn't imagine she had such a forehand, but I found out."

Soon a lot of players found out about Graf's power. But some of Graf's opponents weren't very impressed with her abilities. One of those players was American Tracy Austin. Austin had won the U.S. Open in 1979 and 1981. Two years after winning her second U.S. Open title, Austin was matched against Graf. Austin beat the thirteen-year-old Graf. After the match, Austin was asked about the young German girl. "There are a hundred like her back in the states," Austin said.

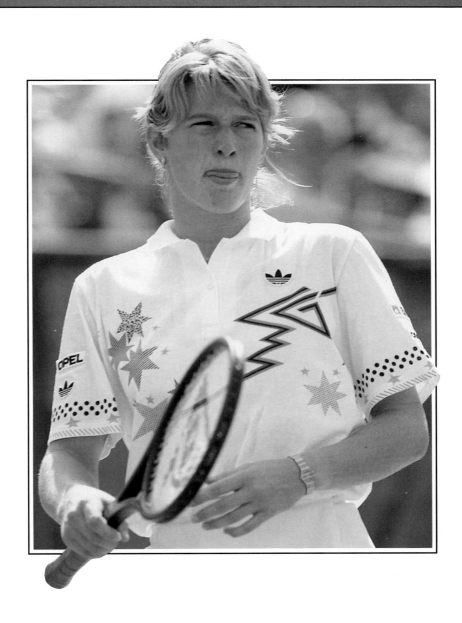

Austin was wrong.
There weren't any tennis players
like Graf back in the United States.
Just four years after playing Austin,
Graf won her first Grand Slam
event, the 1987 French Open. Graf
was only seventeen years old when
she won this tournament. She
became the youngest woman ever
to win the French Open. After
taking the French Open title, Graf
reached the finals of the 1987 All-
England tournament at Wimbledon.
She played Martina Navratilova,
the top player in the world.

Navratilova, who had won seven Wimbledon titles, got her eighth by beating Graf. But even Navratilova could see that Graf was going to be hard to beat in the future. "I don't know how much longer I can hold her off," Martina said. Navratilova did beat Graf in the finals of the 1987 U.S. Open. That was the last time Steffi had to settle for second in a major tournament for more than a year.

Graf won the next five Grand Slam events. When Arantxa Sanchez beat her in the 1989 French Open, it kept Graf from becoming only the fourth player to win six Grand Slam titles in a row. Only Maureen Connolly, Margaret Court, and Navratilova had done that. Some tennis experts called Graf a machine, a player who almost never made a mistake on the court. "Do you like being called a machine?" Graf was asked after one tournament. "I am a machine," Steffi joked.

She had become the most popular German athlete in a long time. She was even more popular than Becker, who no longer lived in Germany. Steffi, though, still called Bruhl home. "Everybody knows me here," Graf said of her hometown. "I don't think I'll ever leave."

Graf had put Bruhl on the map. There are, in fact, two cities named Bruhl in West Germany. One telephone operator was asked to find a phone number in Bruhl. "Bruhl?" the operator asked the caller. "Do you want Steffi's Bruhl or the other one?"

29

Despite her fame and fortune, Graf hasn't changed much. "She's just another player off the court," said Patricia Tarabini. "She is not like, 'I am number one, and you guys get out of here.' She is so plain, so normal." Graf might be plain and normal off the court. On the court, her powerful forehand and amazing foot speed make her one of the best women tennis players ever. And she still has a lot of good years left.